CATS SET I

SIAMESE CATS

Tamara L. Britton
ABDO Publishing Company

visit us at
www.abdopublishing.com

Published by ABDO Publishing Company, 8000 West 78th Street, Edina, Minnesota 55439. Copyright © 2011 by Abdo Consulting Group, Inc. International copyrights reserved in all countries. No part of this book may be reproduced in any form without written permission from the publisher. The Checkerboard Library™ is a trademark and logo of ABDO Publishing Company.

Printed in the United States of America, North Mankato, Minnesota.
042010
092010

 PRINTED ON RECYCLED PAPER

Cover Photo: Photo by Helmi Flick
Interior Photos: Alamy pp. 9, 10; Photo by Helmi Flick pp. 5, 7, 12, 13; iStockphoto pp. 10–11, 14, 16–17; Peter Arnold pp. 19, 21

Editor: Megan M. Gunderson
Art Direction & Cover Design: Neil Klinepier

Library of Congress Cataloging-in-Publication Data

Britton, Tamara L., 1963-
  Siamese cats / Tamara L. Britton.
     p. cm. -- (Cats)
  Includes index.
  ISBN 978-1-61613-401-3
  1. Siamese cat--Juvenile literature. I. Title.
  SF449.S5B75 2011
  636.8'25--dc22
                              2010014955

CONTENTS

LIONS, TIGERS, AND CATS

Around 3,500 years ago, ancient Egyptians began taming African wildcats. These cats hunted rats and mice that feasted on stored grain harvests. Egyptians believed cats were sacred and often worshipped them in temples.

Domestic cats can trace their roots back to these African wildcats. Today, cats are cherished as family members. More than 40 different **breeds** of domestic cats exist worldwide. They come in assorted colors, shapes, and sizes.

All domestic cats belong to the family **Felidae**. This family also includes lions and tigers! In all, there are 37 different cat species.

The Siamese cat

SIAMESE CATS

The **exotic** look of the Siamese cat has fascinated cat lovers for centuries. But where did this marvelous creature come from? A clue is in its name. The Siamese cat was first discovered in Siam! Today, Siam is called Thailand.

In Siam, visitors were charmed by these beautiful cats. Soon, the cats were exported to other countries.

The Siamese came to the United States in 1878. That year, American diplomat David Sickels sent one to U.S. First Lady Lucy Hayes.

Cat lovers continued to import Siamese cats. At the same time, **breeders** worked to perfect the breed. In 1907, a Siamese won the breed's first best in show award at the Michigan Cat Club Show in Detroit, Michigan.

The **Cat Fanciers'
Association (CFA)**
had been formed in
1906. The seal point
Siamese cat was one
of the organization's
original recognized
breeds.

Later, other colors
were recognized. The
group recognized blue
point Siamese in
1934. Chocolate
points were recognized
in 1952, followed by
lilac points in 1955.

*There are more seal point
Siamese cats at cat shows
than any other color.*

QUALITIES

What are you doing? Your Siamese will want to know! These cats are curious. So, they need owners who can give them lots of attention. They appreciate feline companions, too!

These intelligent cats like to be around their people. They are loving and affectionate. Siamese cats will sit on your lap, on your bed, or on the book you are reading!

Siamese cats are playful and outgoing. They will not tolerate being ignored. In fact, these cats are very talkative. They will use a variety of cries to let you know exactly what they think!

Scientists have identified 16 different cat vocalizations. Siamese cats appear to know and enjoy using them all!

8

COAT AND COLOR

Siamese kittens are born white. Their points gradually gain color as they get older.

It is easy to recognize a Siamese cat. Its short, silky coat is **uniquely** colored. The fur on the cat's points is darker than the rest of the body. The points are the cat's ears, face, legs, and tail.

A Siamese cat may be one of four colors. A seal point cat has a cream-colored body. Its seal brown points look almost black. A blue point cat has a bluish white body. Its points are slate blue.

Chocolate point Siamese have ivory bodies with chocolate brown points. Lilac point cats have white bodies. Their points are pinkish gray.

No matter their color, all Siamese cats have blue eyes.

SIZE

Siamese cats are medium sized. Males range from 10 to 12 pounds (4.5 to 5.5 kg). Females are smaller. They weigh 8 to 10 pounds (3.5 to 4.5 kg).

Years of selective breeding have perfected the wedge-shaped head.

The Siamese has a long, wedge-shaped head on a long, slender neck. The large, almond-shaped eyes angle down toward the nose and up toward the ears. The ears are wide at the base. They taper up to pointed tips.

A long, graceful body makes the Siamese

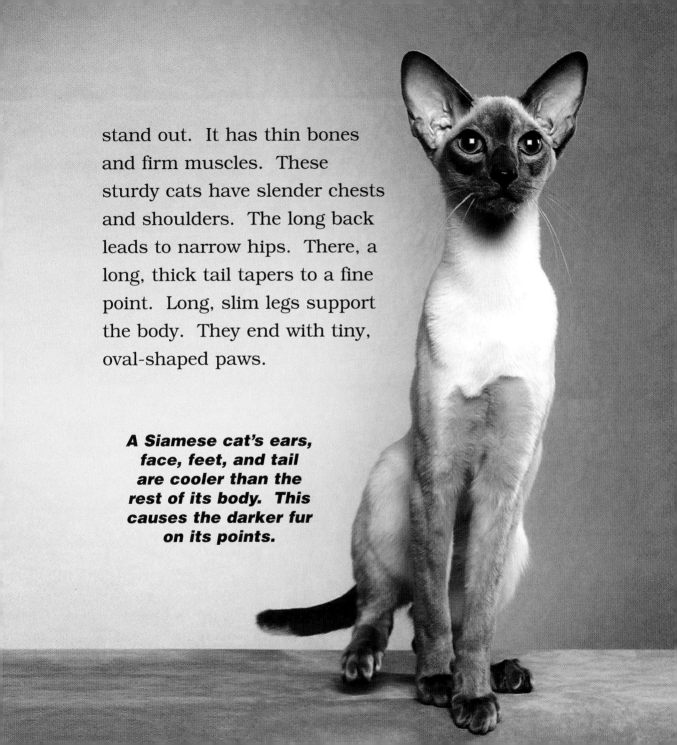

stand out. It has thin bones and firm muscles. These sturdy cats have slender chests and shoulders. The long back leads to narrow hips. There, a long, thick tail tapers to a fine point. Long, slim legs support the body. They end with tiny, oval-shaped paws.

A Siamese cat's ears, face, feet, and tail are cooler than the rest of its body. This causes the darker fur on its points.

CARE

Cats use their rough tongues to clean their fur. A Siamese can keep its short coat clean. However, you should groom it with a brush occasionally to remove loose hair. This will keep the cat from forming hairballs. Grooming also provides an opportunity to give this social cat extra attention!

Cats have a natural instinct to bury their waste. So, you can train your Siamese to use a **litter box**. Keep the box in a quiet place away from the cat's food and water. Do not forget to remove waste from the box every day!

As hunters, cats enjoy the outdoors. There, they sharpen their claws on trees. But, cats are safer and healthier when they live indoors. A scratching post will allow your Siamese to sharpen its claws without damaging furniture and carpet.

Toys will bring out your cat's playful nature. A ball or a catnip mouse will provide lots of fun. Your Siamese may even play fetch!

Sometimes, even indoor cats develop health problems. It is important to visit the veterinarian once a year. He or she can provide checkups and **vaccines**. The veterinarian can also **spay** or **neuter** your cat.

Your veterinarian can teach you ways to prevent medical problems in your cat.

FEEDING

Cats are carnivores. So, they need to eat meat as part of a healthy diet. Your Siamese will need cat food that contains beef, poultry, or fish. Feeding your cat a quality commercial food will give it all the **nutrients** it needs.

The three kinds of commercial cat food are dry, semimoist, and canned. The label will tell you how much and how often to feed your cat. Always put your cat's food in a clean bowl.

All cats need plenty of fresh water. Make sure to always have some available in a bowl. You can also give your cat an occasional treat. But don't be too generous! Indoor cats can easily become overweight. If you are concerned about your cat's weight, check with your veterinarian about its feeding schedule.

Kittens need several small meals each day. Adult cats eat fewer times a day.

KITTENS

A female Siamese cat is **pregnant** for about 63 to 65 days. She usually gives birth to four kittens in each **litter**. The kittens will drink milk from their mother for about five weeks.

The kittens are born blind and deaf. They begin to see and hear when they are two weeks old. After about three weeks, the kittens are better able to see and hear. They begin to play and explore their surroundings. And, their teeth are coming in!

Siamese kittens should be handled gently every day. This will create calm, friendly pets. When the kittens are 12 to 16 weeks old, they are ready to be adopted.

Cats are social animals. They enjoy the companionship of other cats in the house.

BUYING A KITTEN

Have you decided a Siamese is the right cat for you? Well, you're in good company! The Siamese is the fourth most popular **breed** in the **CFA**.

When you are ready to get a kitten, you must decide if you want a show cat or a pet cat. The best place to begin looking for a show-quality kitten is a reputable breeder. Cat shows are also good places to look.

The cost of a Siamese kitten will depend on its color and **pedigree**. A kitten from award-winning parents can be very expensive. Another option for finding a Siamese is visiting shelters and rescue organizations. They may have Siamese cats that need loving forever homes.

When choosing a kitten, check it closely for signs of good health. The cat's ears, nose, mouth, and fur should be clean. Its eyes should be bright and clear.

Siamese cats love their people and want to be near them. They are great companion cats!

Choose your new friend carefully! A well cared for Siamese cat will be a loving companion for 15 to 20 years.

GLOSSARY

breed - a group of animals sharing the same ancestors and appearance. A breeder is a person who raises animals. Raising animals is often called breeding them.

Cat Fanciers' Association (CFA) - a group that sets the standards for judging all breeds of cats.

domestic - tame, especially relating to animals.

exotic - strikingly, excitingly, or mysteriously different or unusual.

Felidae (FEHL-uh-dee) - the scientific Latin name for the cat family. Members of this family are called felids. They include domestic cats, lions, tigers, leopards, jaguars, cougars, wildcats, lynx, and cheetahs.

litter - all of the kittens born at one time to a mother cat.

litter box - a box filled with cat litter, which is similar to sand. Cats use litter boxes to bury their waste.

neuter (NOO-tuhr) - to remove a male animal's reproductive organs.

nutrient - a substance found in food and used in the body. It promotes growth, maintenance, and repair.

pedigree - a record of an animal's ancestors.

pregnant - having one or more babies growing within the body.

spay - to remove a female animal's reproductive organs.

unique - being the only one of its kind.

vaccine (vak-SEEN) - a shot given to prevent illness or disease.

WEB SITES

To learn more about Siamese cats, visit ABDO Publishing Company on the World Wide Web at **www.abdopublishing.com**. Web sites about Siamese cats are featured on our Book Links page. These links are routinely monitored and updated to provide the most current information available.

INDEX